**Authentic Transcriptions
by Jack Morer**

Wise Publications
London / New York / Paris / Sydney / Copenhagen / Madrid

Exclusive Distributors:
Music Sales Limited
14-15 Berners Street,
London W1T 3LJ, England.

Music Sales Pty Limited
20 Resolution Drive,
Caringbah, NSW 2229,
Australia.

Order No. AM92677
ISBN 0-7119-4791-0
This book © Copyright 1994 by
Wise Publications.

Art direction by Michael Bell Design.
Photographs courtesy of
London Features International and Retna.

Your Guarantee of Quality:
As publishers, we strive to produce every
book to the highest commercial standards.
This book has been carefully designed to
make playing from it a real pleasure.
Throughout, the printing and binding have
been planned to ensure a sturdy, attractive
publication which should give years of enjoyment.

If your copy fails to meet our high standards,
please inform us and we will gladly replace it.

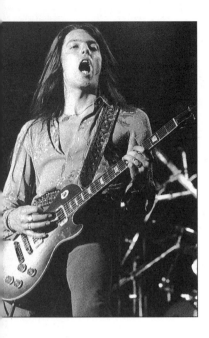

Are You Ready

Words & Music by Philip Parris Lynott, Brian Michael Downey, William Scott Gorham & Brian Robertson

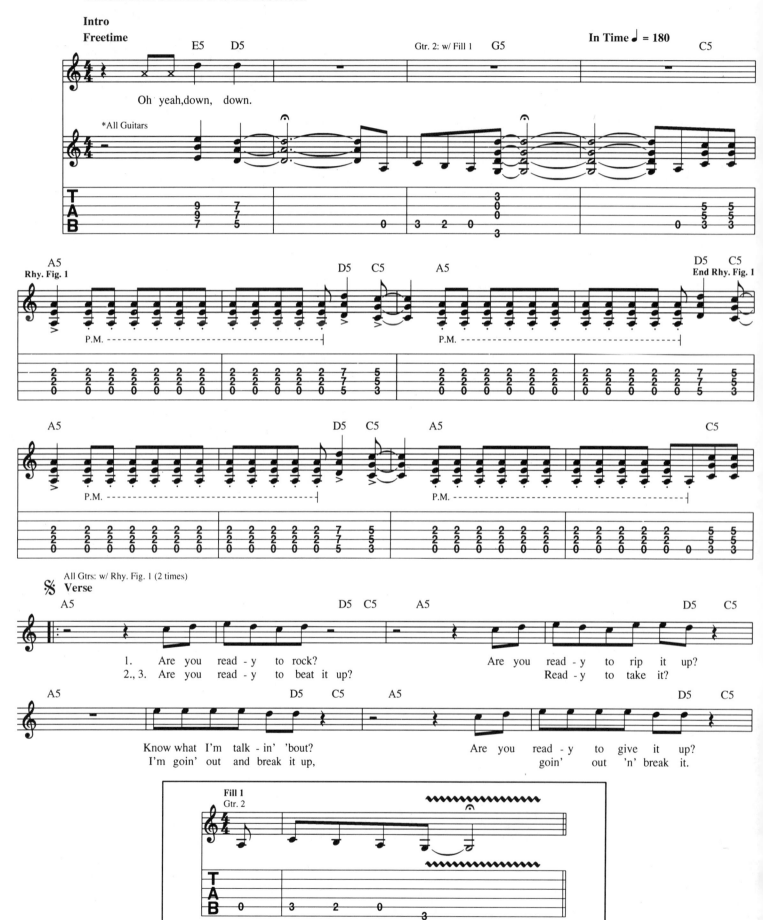

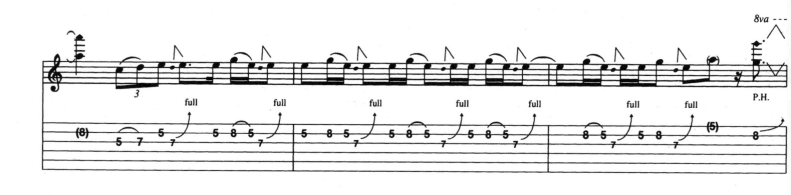

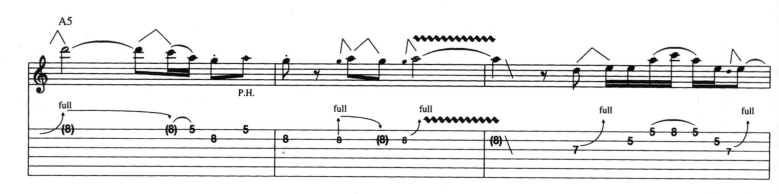

9

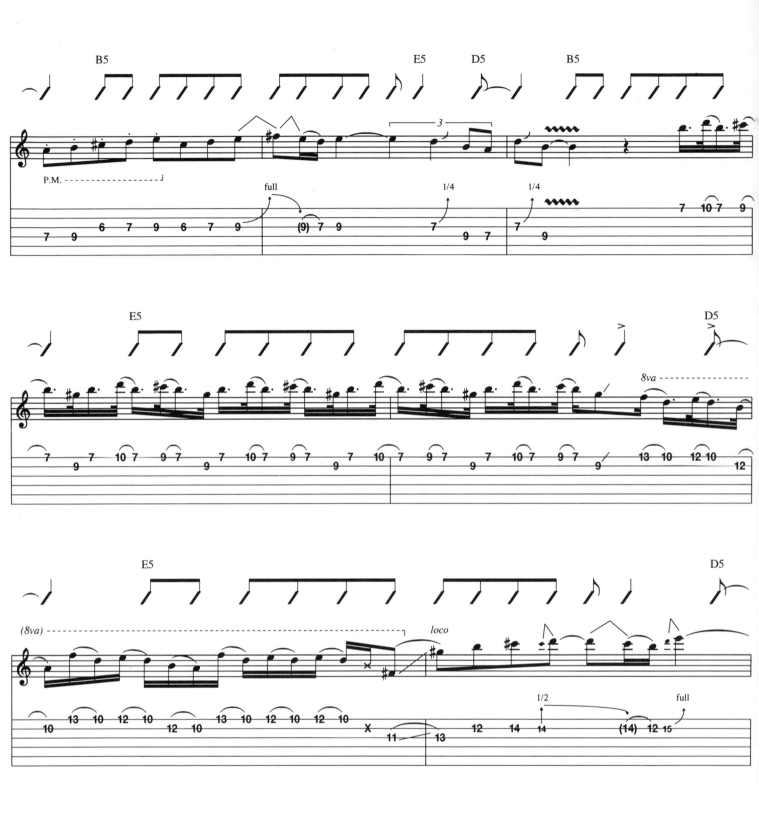

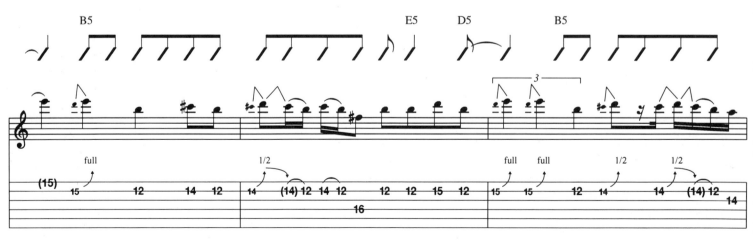

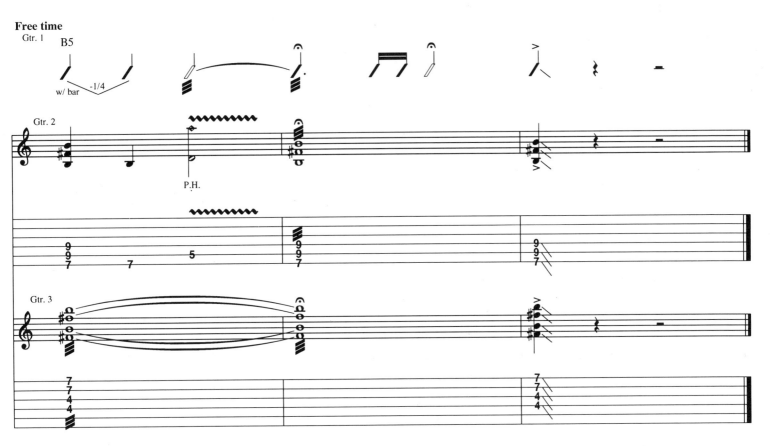

Bad Reputation

**Words & Music by Philip Parris Lynott,
Brian Michael Downey & William Scott Gorham**

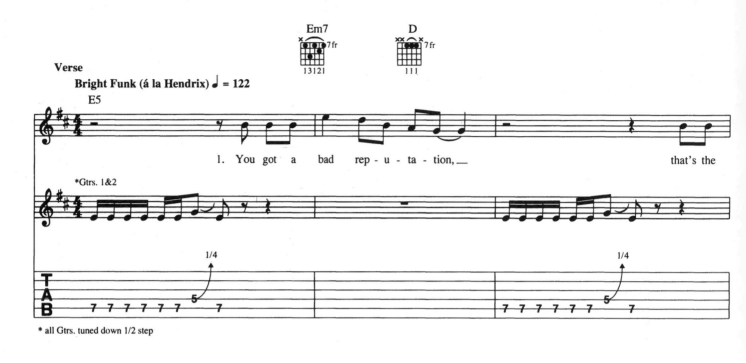

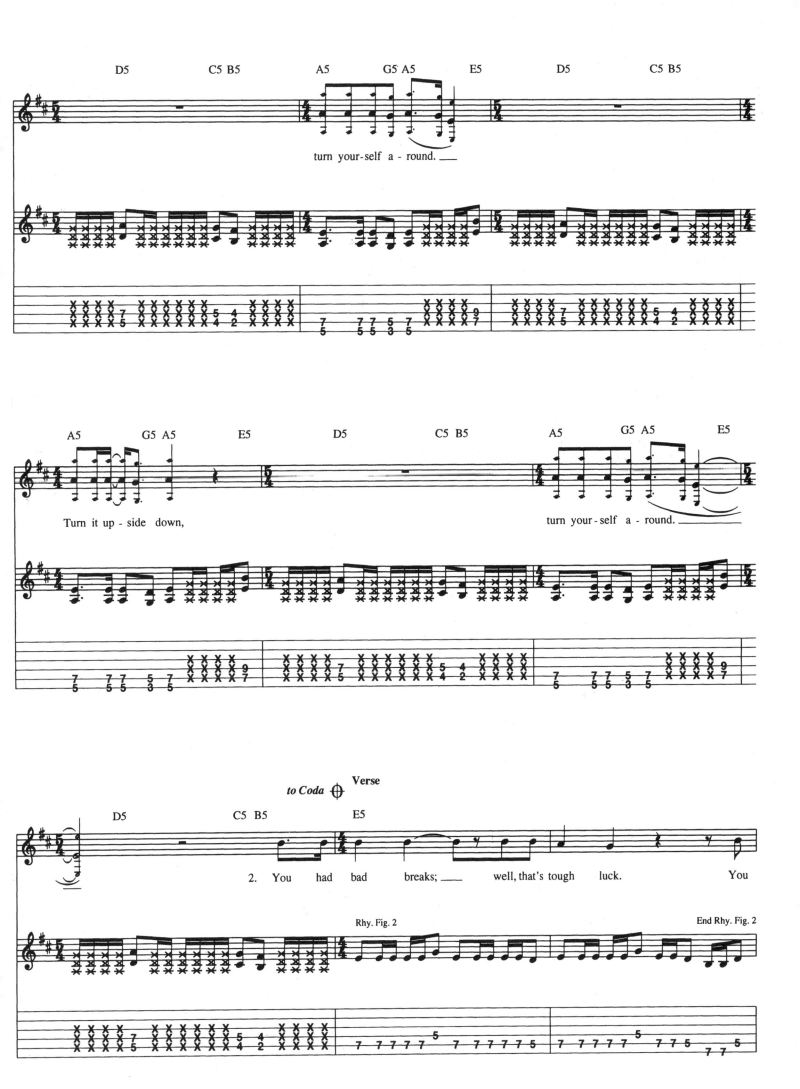

turn your-self a - round. ___

Turn it up - side down,   turn your-self a - round. ___

to Coda ⊕   **Verse**

2. You had bad breaks; ___ well, that's tough luck. ___ You

Rhy. Fig. 2   End Rhy. Fig. 2

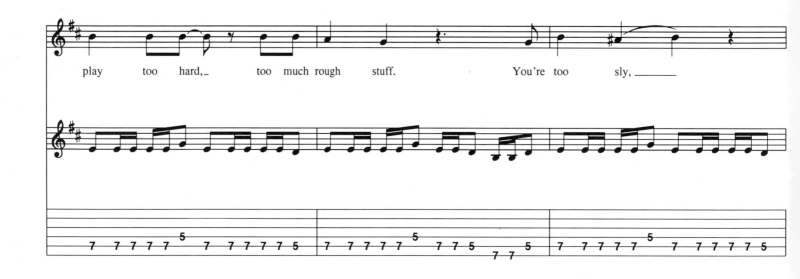

play   too   hard,__   too much rough   stuff.   You're too   sly,_____

so   cold._____   That   bad__   re - pu - ta - tion   has   made   you   old. __

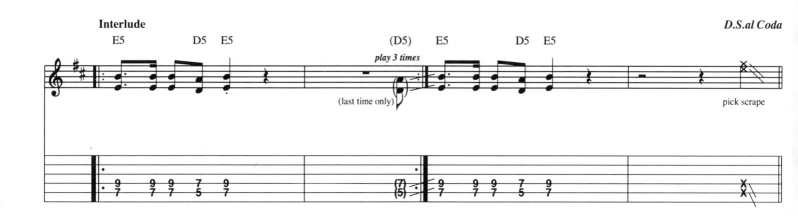

Interlude

D.S.al Coda

E5   D5   E5   (D5)   E5   D5   E5

play 3 times

(last time only)   pick scrape

Solo

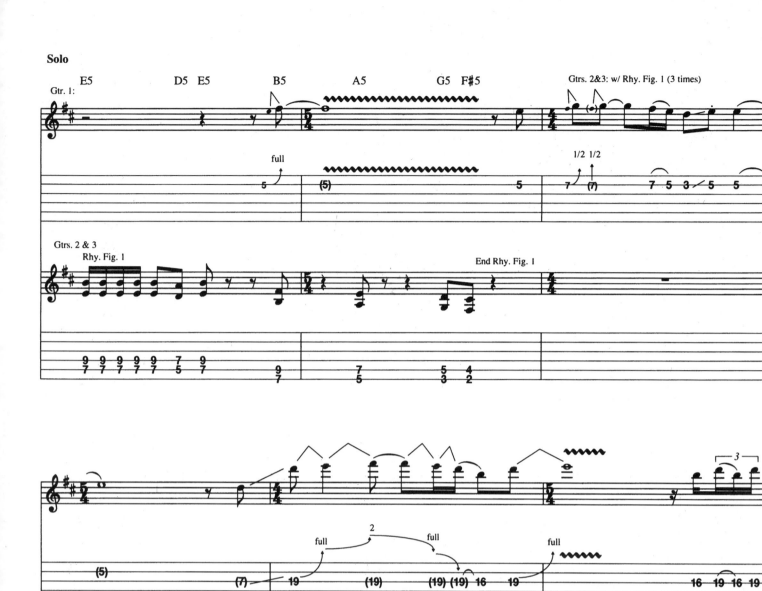

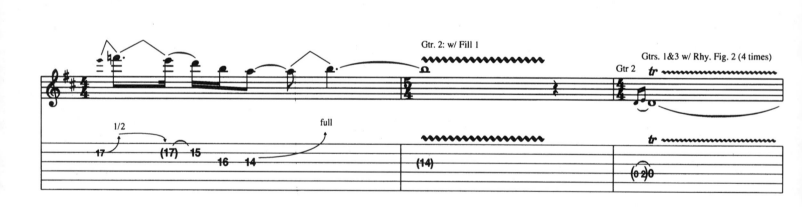

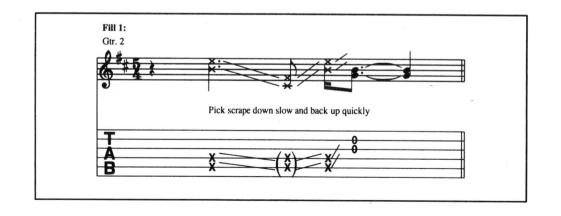

Fill 1:
Gtr. 2

Pick scrape down slow and back up quickly

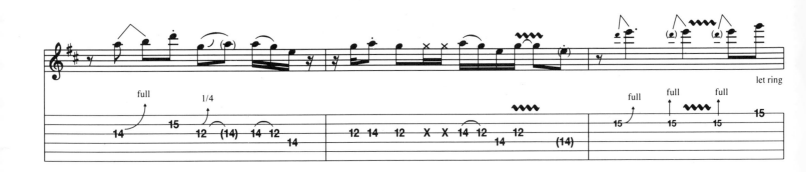

let ring

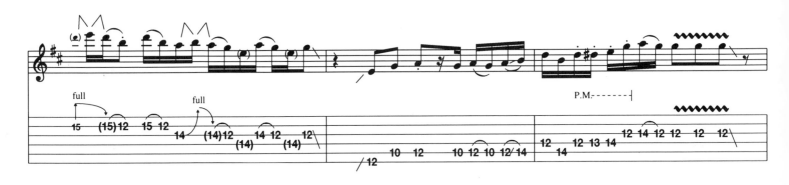

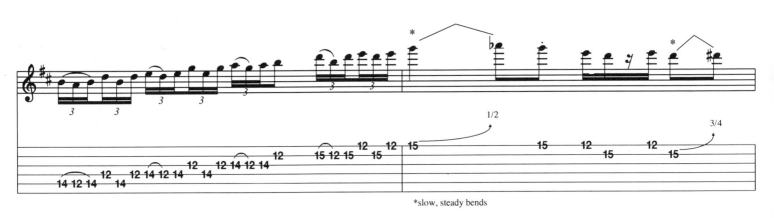

*slow, steady bends

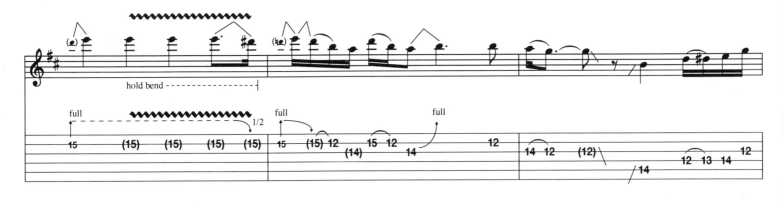

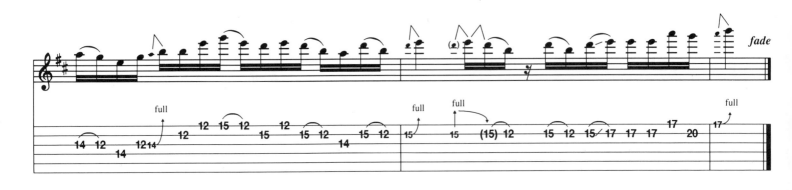

The Boys Are Back In Town

Words & Music by Philip Parris Lynott

* 1st time only

let ring

Fill 1
Gtr 2:

boys ___ are back in town. __ The boys ___ are back in town. __ The boys ___ are back in town. __

The boys

Gtr. 3 tacet   N.C.

___ are back in town. __

Bridge

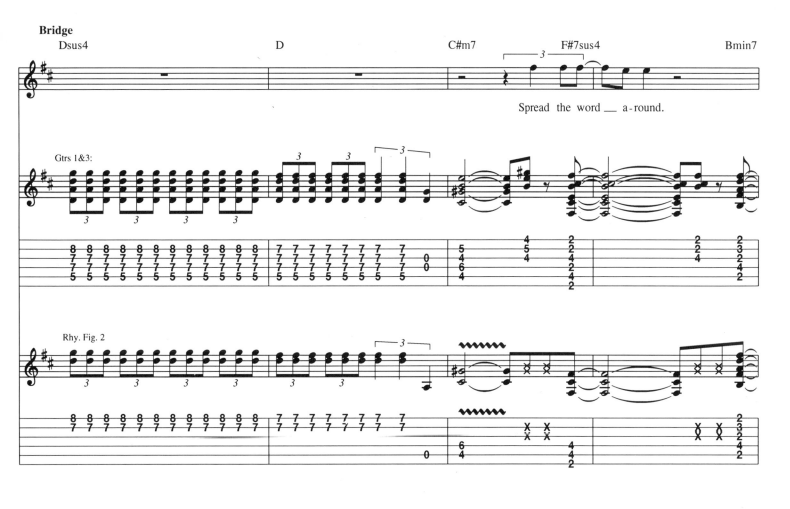

Spread the word __ a-round.

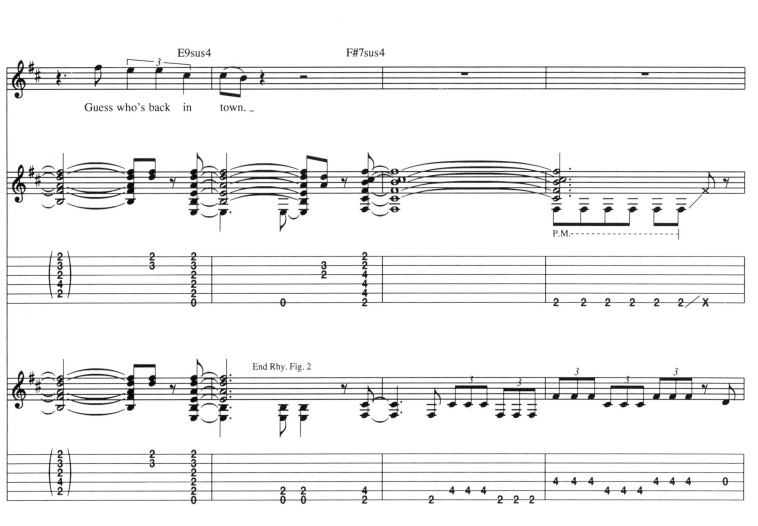

Guess who's back in town. _

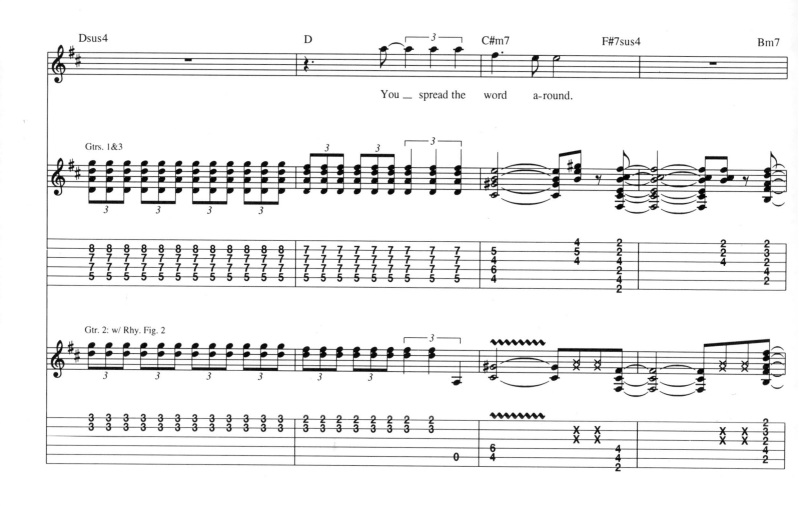

You __ spread the word a-round.

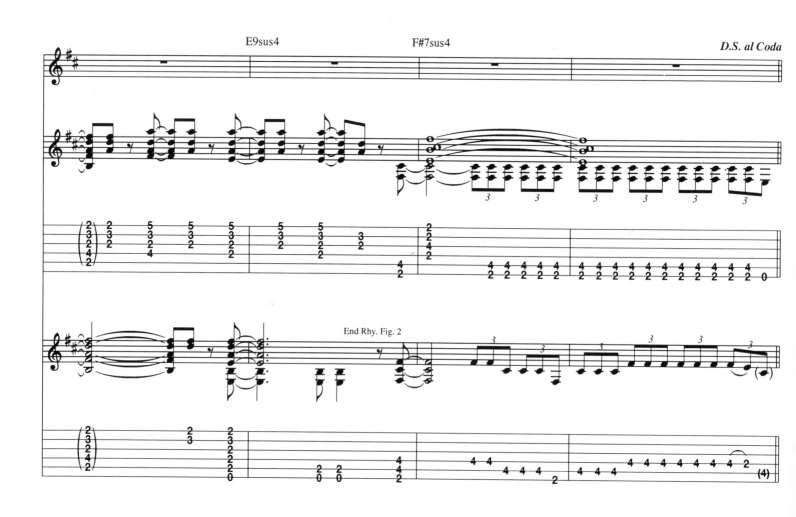

boys _ are back in town. _ The boys _ are back in town. _ *(Spread the word a - round.)* The

boys _ are back in town. _ The boys _ are back in town _ *(The boys are back.* *The boys are back.)*

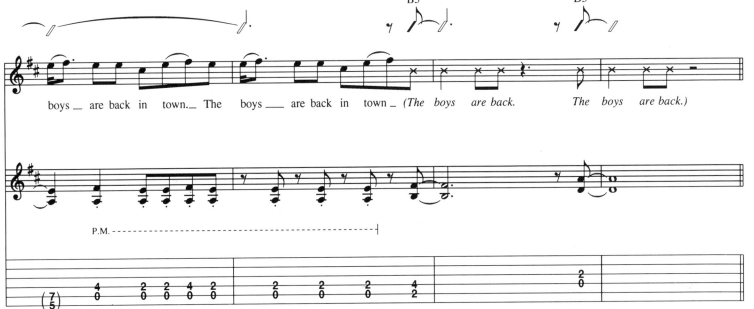

The boys ___ are back ___ in town ___ a - gain. ___

'Been hang - in' down ___ at Di - no's ___

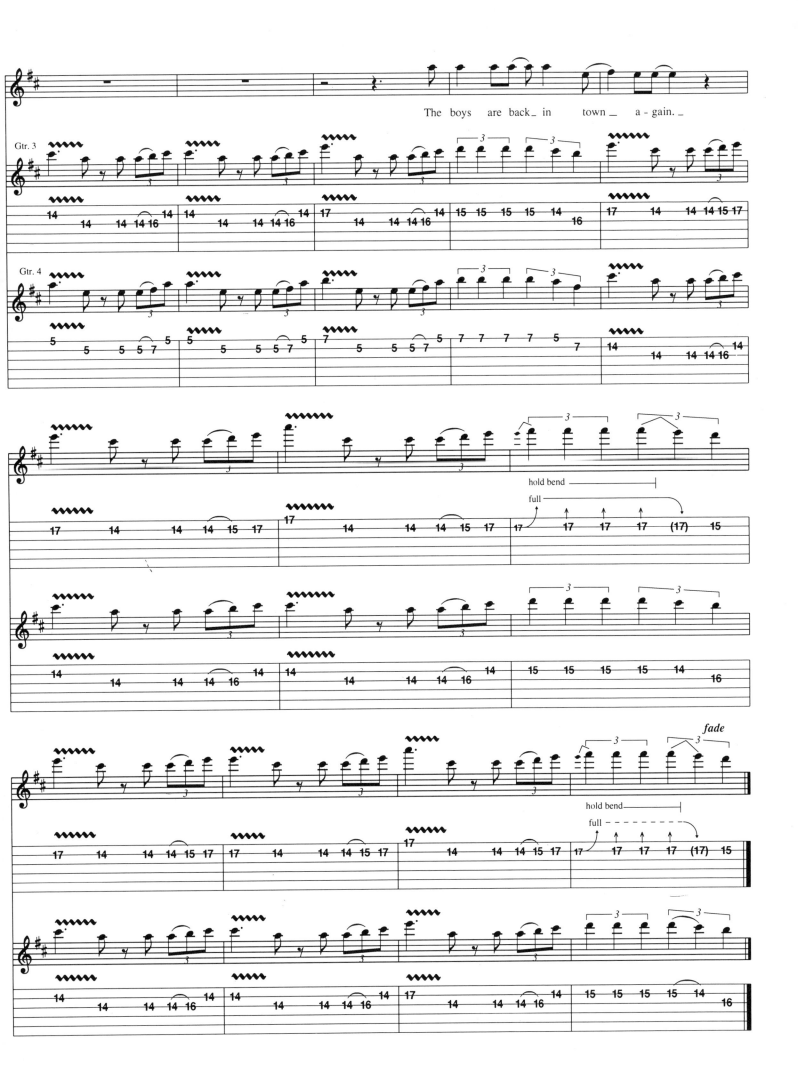

The boys are back_ in   town _   a - gain. _

Chinatown

Words & Music by Philip Parris Lynott,
Brian Michael Downey, William Scott Gorham & Snowy White

*During the verses, Gtr. 2 plays this riff as shown in fill 2.

live with the dy - ing __ down in old Chi - na-town. In
laugh-in', they are cryin', 'cause they won't be __ back. Oh no, you
Look at the dy - in', there is no relief. there is

Gtr. 2: 1st time w/ Fill 3
2nd time w/ Fill 6
3rd time w/ Fill 9

Chi - na - town,_ you bet-ter look a - round. __
don't come back, back from Chi-na-town.
no be-liefs down in Chi-na-town.

Gtr. 2: 1st, 2nd time w/ Fill 4
3rd time w/ Fill 10

Rhy. Fig. 2   End Rhy. Fig. 2

Man, you

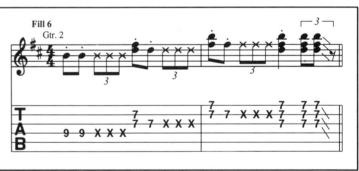

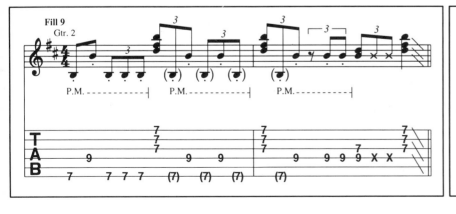

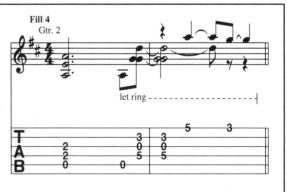

Bridge

First Guitar Solo

E5

Ha, ha, ha, ha, ha, ha, ha, ha, ha.

hold note 'till it fades

Cowboy Song

Words & Music by Philip Parris Lynott & Brian Michael Downey

* use these notes later in the song
  as part of Rhy. figures 2&3

1. I am just a cow - boy, lone - some on the trail.
2. I was took in Texas, I did not know her name.

Lord, _ I'm just think - in' 'bout _ a cer - tain fe - male.
Lord, _ all these southern girls, they seem the same.

The

Fill 3

Fill 7

Fill 4

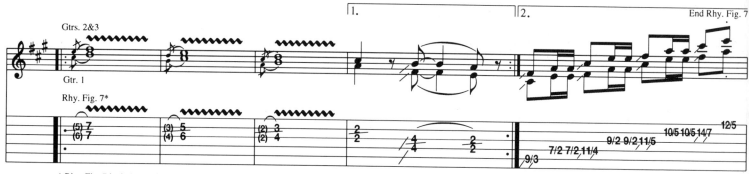

* Rhy. Fig. 7 includes all Gtrs. w/ repeats and 1st and 2nd endings (8 meas. long)

It's O. K.   a - mi - go,   just let me go   ri - din' in the ro -

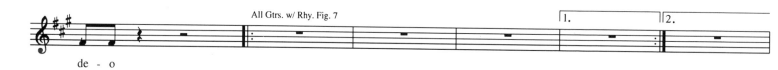

de - o

Solo 2

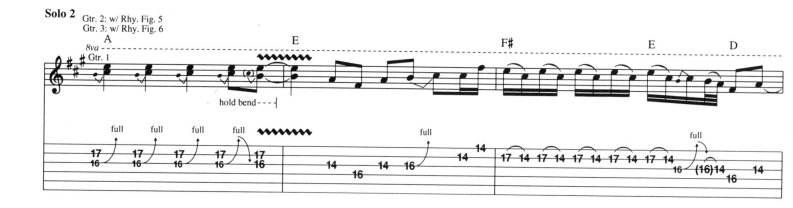

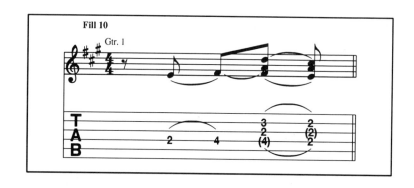

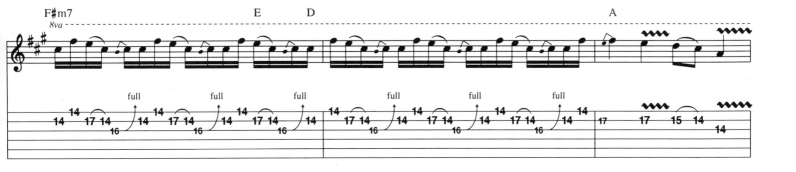

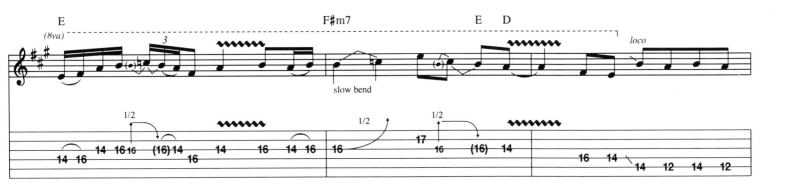

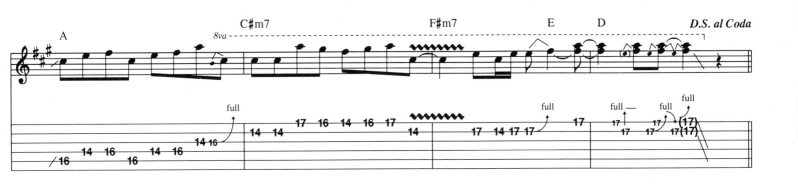

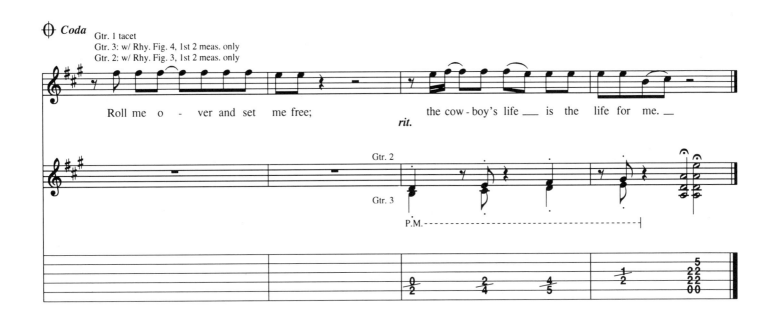

Roll me o - ver and set me free; the cow - boy's life __ is the life for me. __

Dancing In The Moonlight

Words & Music by Philip Parris Lynott

Intro

Asbury Shuffle ♩ = 144

When I

Verse

passed you   in the door - way,   well, you   took   me with   a glance. ___
three   o'clock   in the   morn - ing   and I'm   on   the   streets again.

*Gtrs. 1, 2 & 3
Rhy. Fig. 1

* Gtrs 1 & 2 are electric. Gtr 3 is acoustic.

I should-'ve took ___   that   last   bus   home, ___   but I
I disobeyed   another   warning,   I

Gtr. 2: w/Fill 1, 1st and 2nd time

Fill 1
Gtr 2

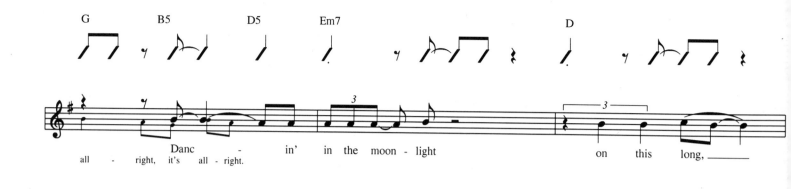

Danc - in' in the moon - light on this long,

all - right, it's all - right.

To Coda

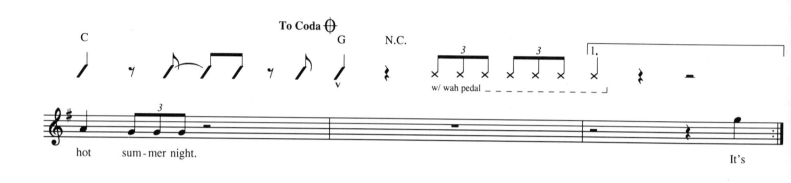

w/ wah pedal

hot sum - mer night.

It's

2. Gtrs. 1 & 3 tacet

Bridge

Em

C

Gtr. 2: (w/ bass)

G

Em

C

And I'm walk - in' home.

Gtr. Solo
Gtrs. 1, 2 & 3: w/ Rhy. Fig. 1

* slide down and back up in one motion.

Do Anything You Want To

Words & Music by Philip Parris Lynott

* all Gtrs. tuned down 1/2 step.

51

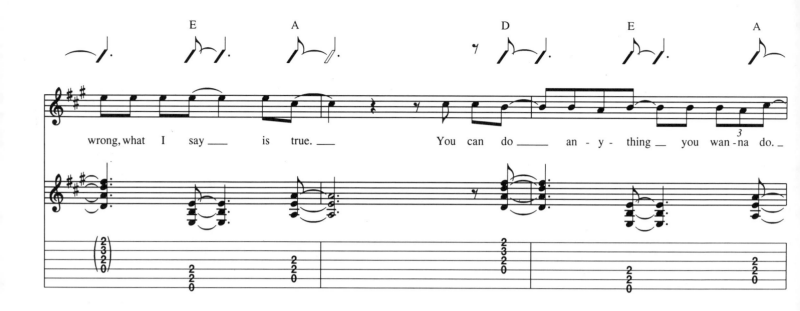

wrong, what I say ___ is true. ___ You can do ___ an-y-thing ___ you wan-na do.___

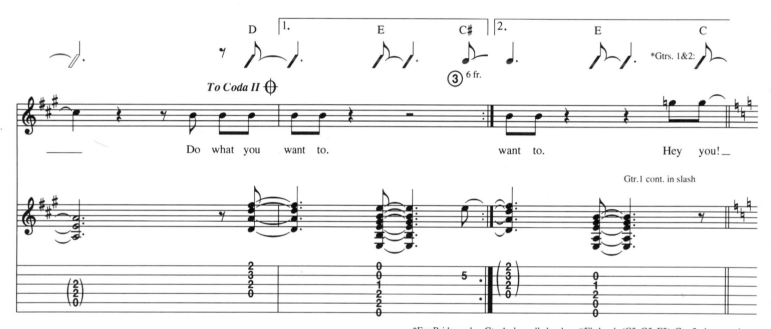

Do what you want to. want to. Hey you!___

Gtr.1 cont. in slash

*For Bridge only - Gtr. 1 plays all chords as "5" chords (C5, G5, F5). Gtr. 2 play as written.

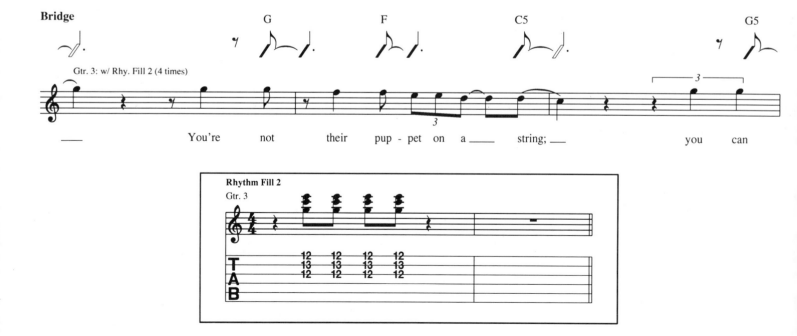

You're not their pup-pet on a ___ string; ___ you can

do ev - ry - thing. ___   It's true, ___   if you real - ly   want to,

you can do an - y - thing you want.

Just   like   I   do.

D.S. al Coda

Coda

You __

want.

A

⊕ *Coda II*

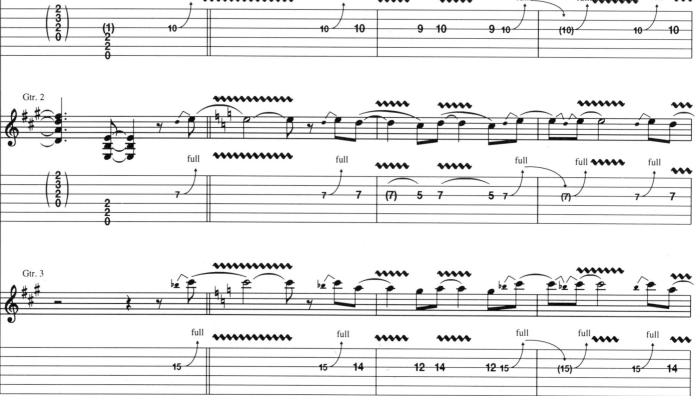

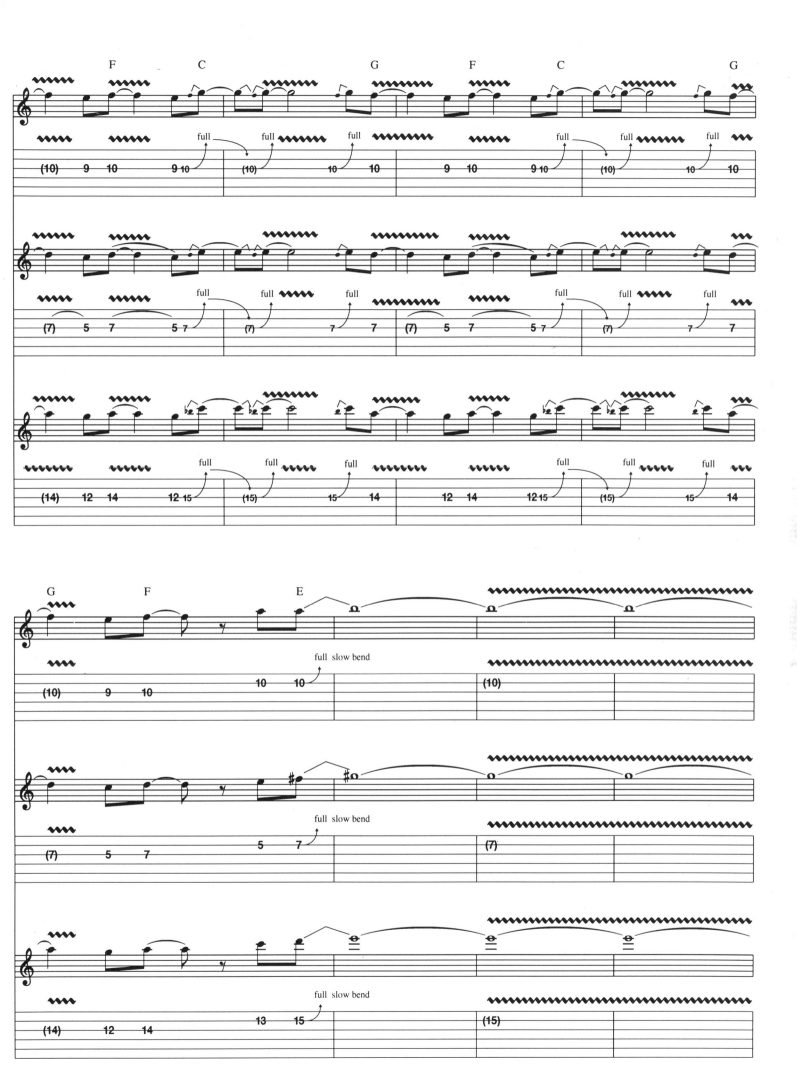

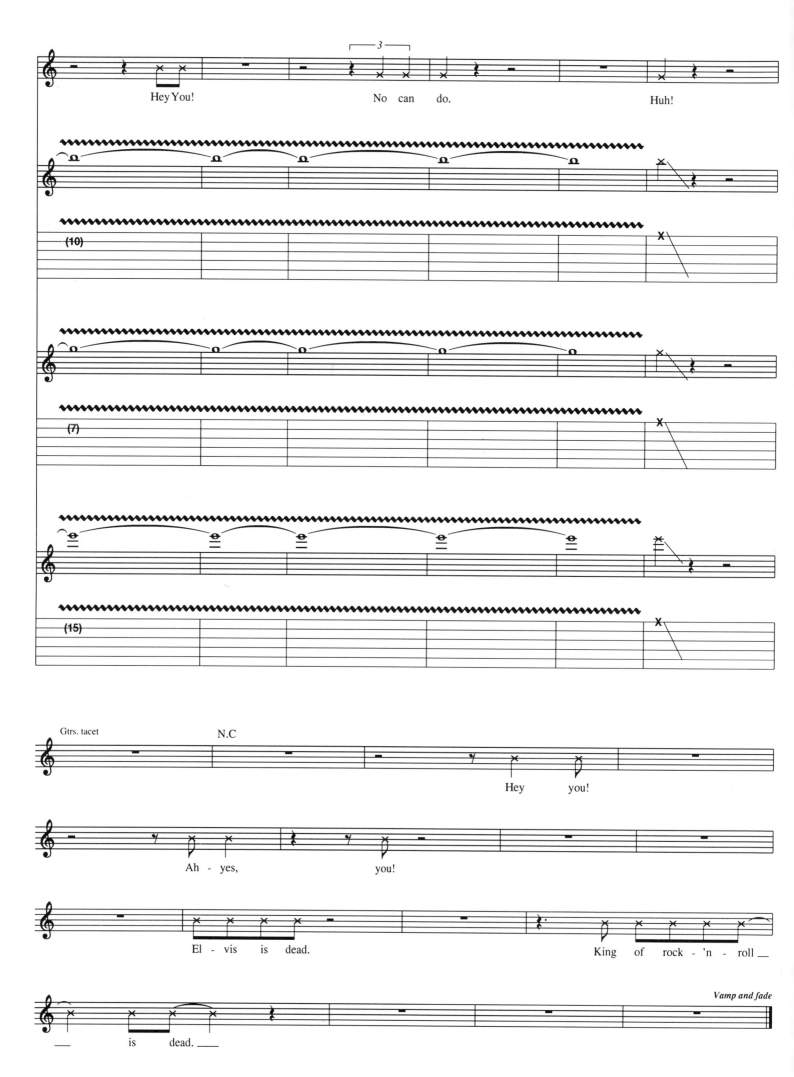

Hey You!   No can do.   Huh!

(10)

(7)

(15)

Gtrs. tacet   N.C

Hey   you!

Ah - yes,   you!

El - vis is dead.   King of rock - 'n - roll __

Vamp and fade

__ is dead. __

Don't Believe A Word

Words & Music by Philip Parris Lynott

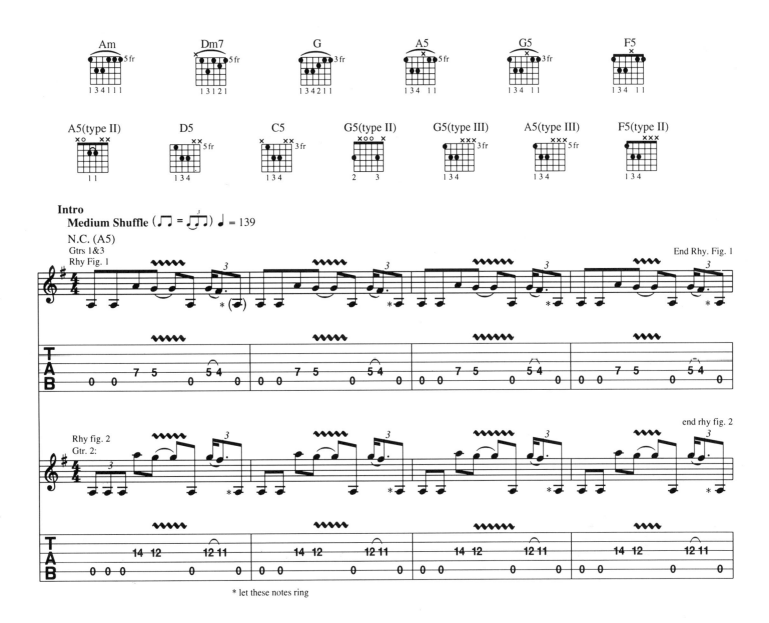

* let these notes ring

Don't be-lieve me if I

Gtr. 1: w/ Rhy. Fig. 1 (1st 3 measures)
Gtr. 2: w/ Rhy. Fig. 2 (1st 3 measures)
Gtr. 3:

A5(type II)
Gtrs. 1&3

Bridge

word, / word, / for words are so eas-i-ly spo-ken, / 'cause words can tell lies. / And your / And lies

heart, it's just like that pro-mise: meant to be bro-ken. / Don't be-lieve me if I
are no com-fort when there's tears in your eyes.

(vocal tacet 1st time)

Solo

Am   Dm   G

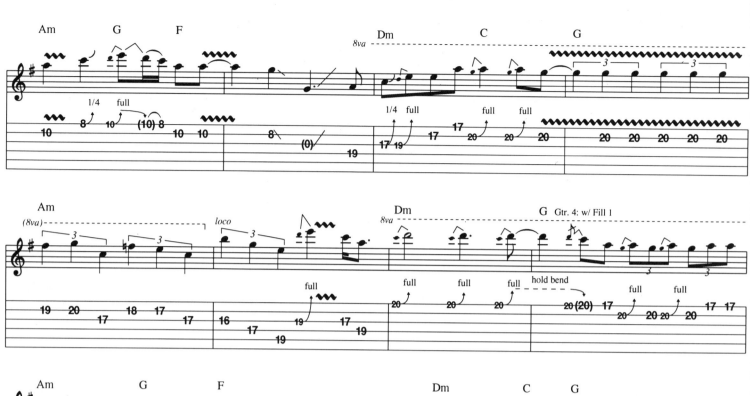

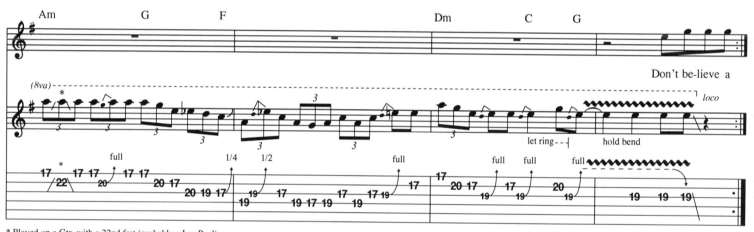

* Played on a Gtr. with a 22nd fret (probably a Les Paul).

*Gtr. 4 is buried in the mix during this section and is approximated for these 8 bars

60

it,   not a sin-gle word. ___   Hey   don' _ cha.

Jailbreak

Words & Music by Philip Parris Lynott

*Gtrs. 1 & 2
*Gtr. 3

*All Gtrs. tuned down 1/2 step

The lyrics shown in the Verse:

1. To-night there's gon-na be a jail break somewhere in this town.
2. To-night there's gon-na be trou-ble. Some of us won't sur-
3. To-night there's gon-na be a break-out into the ci-ty zones.

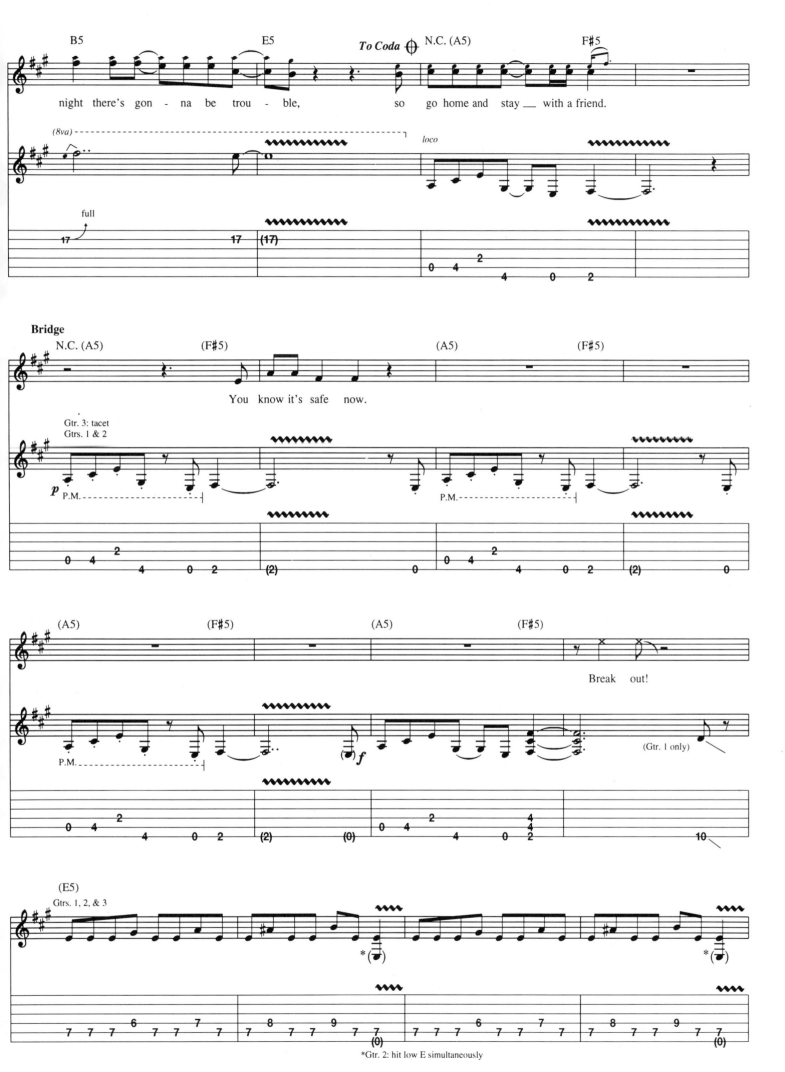

night there's gon - na be trou - ble,   so   go home and   stay __ with a friend.

Bridge

You know it's safe   now.

Gtr. 3: tacet
Gtrs. 1 & 2

Break   out!

(Gtr. 1 only)

Gtrs. 1, 2, & 3

*(♪)   *(♪)

*Gtr. 2: hit low E simultaneously

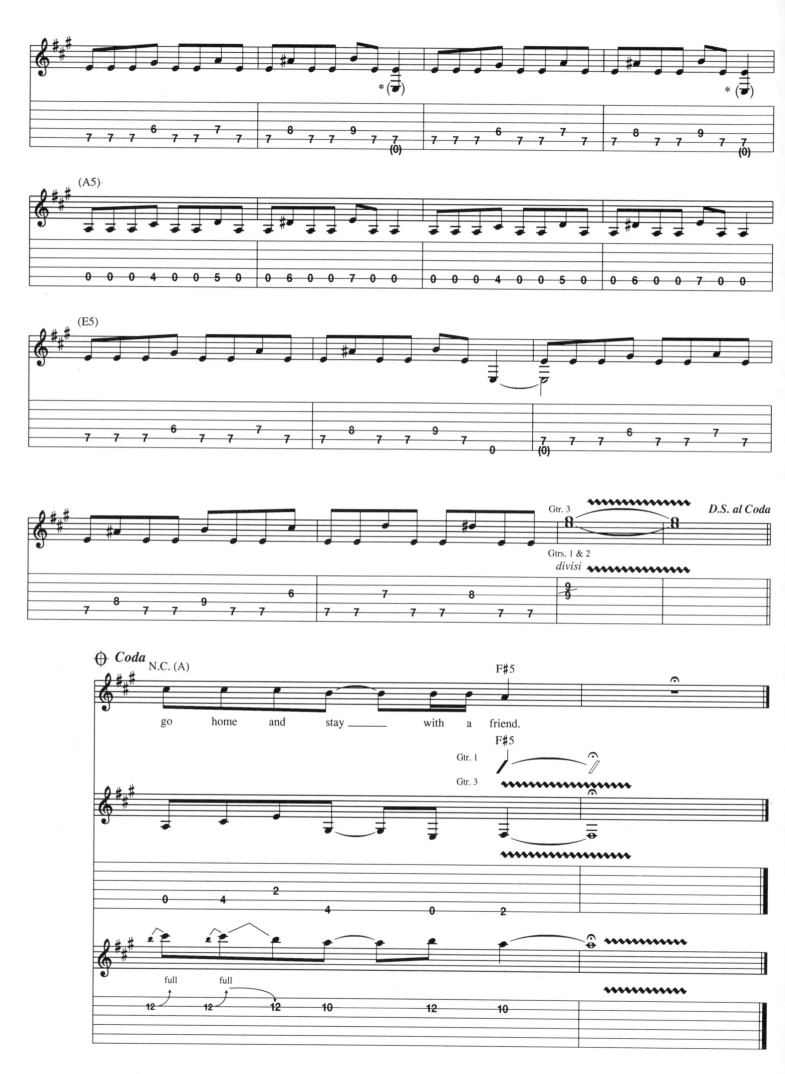

Killer On The Loose

Words & Music by Philip Parris Lynott

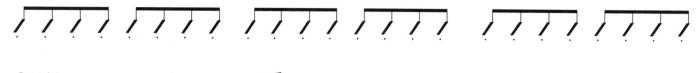

Gtrs. 1 & 2

C#5 D5 C#5

Verse

Gtr. 3

E5   D5   ⑤ 4 fr.   ⑥ 5 fr.   D5   ⑤ 4 fr.
            C#   A   E5   C#   E5

1. Some peo - ple, they call me   Jack. _____   Some peo - ple, they call me in - sane. _____   I'm

2. I'm not try - in' to be   nas - ty.   I'm not try - in' to make you scared.

*1: This passage sounds like it is created by playing the first slide up as shown, with the next 6 repeats coming from a digital delay pedal set
on approximately 250 m.s. with infinite repeats.

*2: This passage sounds like an overdubbed slide guitar with a long, steady gliss from A up to E.

73

Sarah

Words & Music by Philip Parris Lynott & Gary Moore

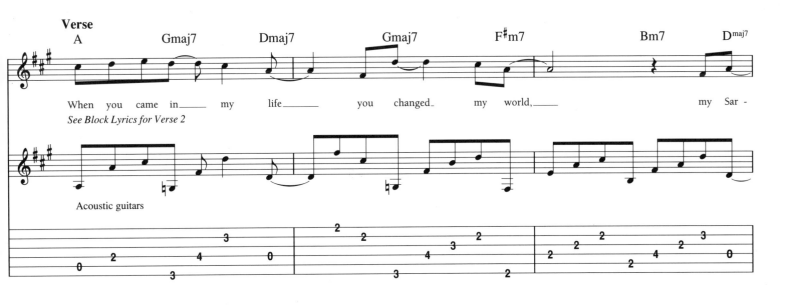

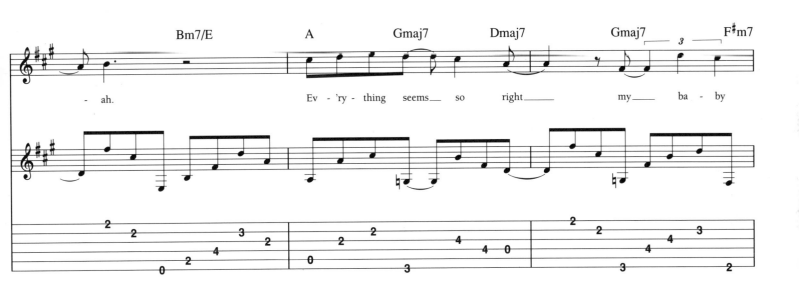

to know___ you hold___ my heart___ so don't___ let go.___

You are all I need___ to live___ my love ___ to you___ I'll give.___

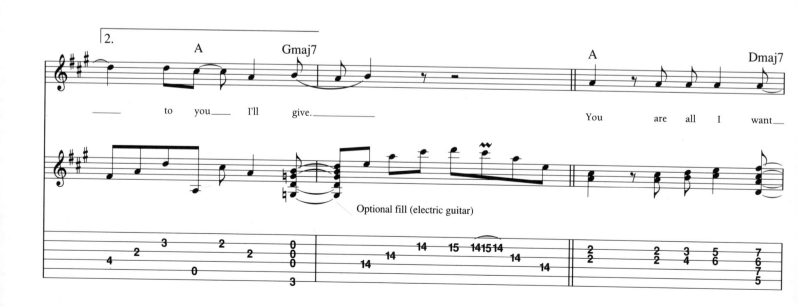

___ to you___ I'll give.___

You are all I want___

Optional fill (electric guitar)

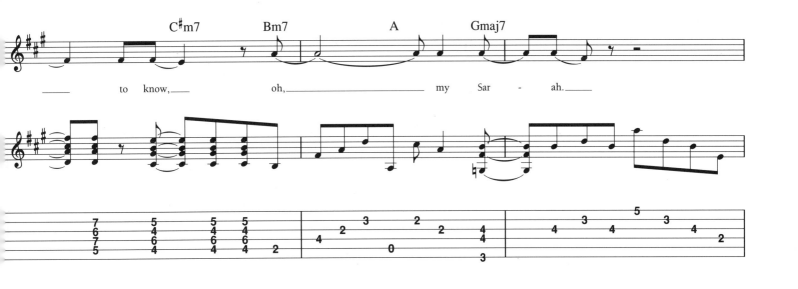

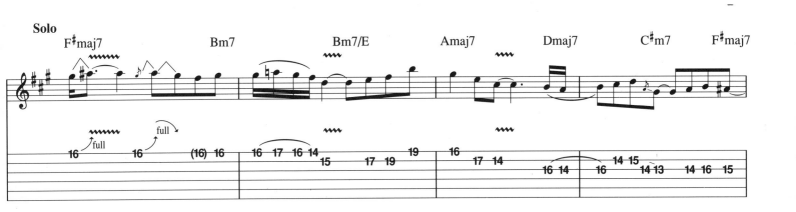

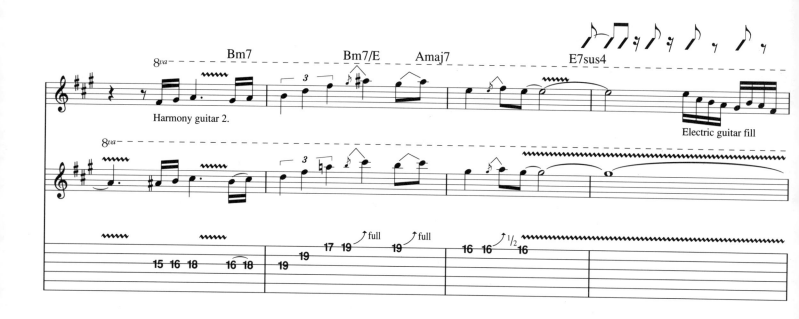

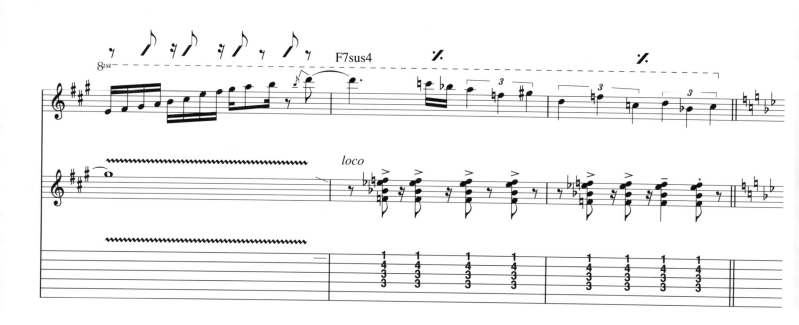

Chorus

You are all I want_____ to know,___ you hold___ my heart___ so don't___

78

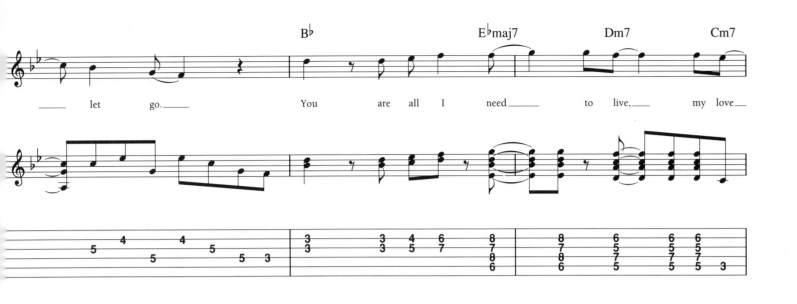

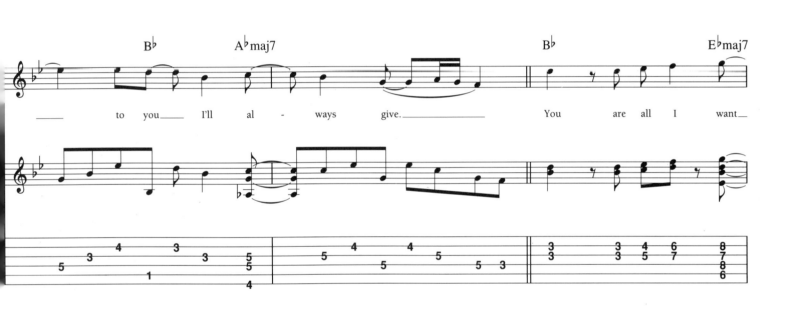

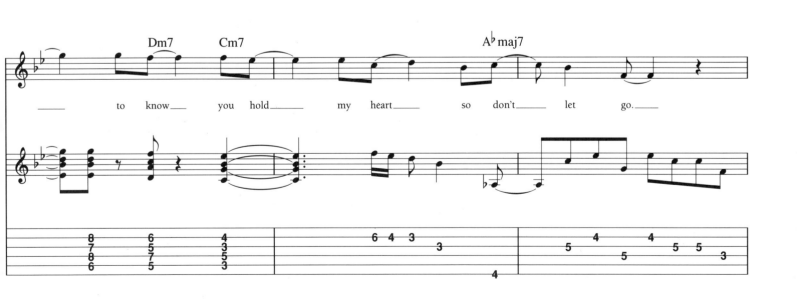

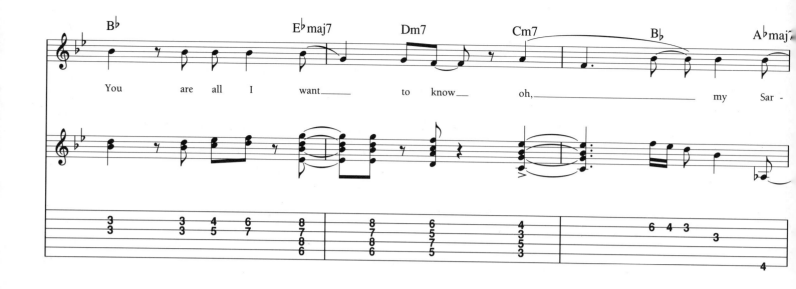

You are all I want____ to know____ oh,_____ my Sar-

- ah.____ Yes you change my____ style with your ba - by's____ smile,

See Block Lyrics to fade.

oh, Sar - ah. Child like charm that keep__

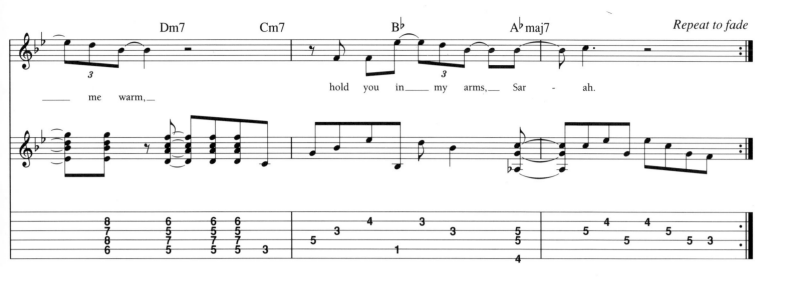

Verse 2: When you begin to smile
You change my style, my Sarah
When I look in your eyes
I see my prize, my Sarah.

You are all I want to know
You hold my heart so don't let go
You are all I need to live
My love to you I'll give.

Lyrics on repeat to fade:

Change my world
My baby girl, Sarah,
You're all I want to know
Don't let 'em go.
No, no, no, no...

Thunder And Lightning

Words & Music by Philip Parris Lynott & Brian Michael Downey

A5

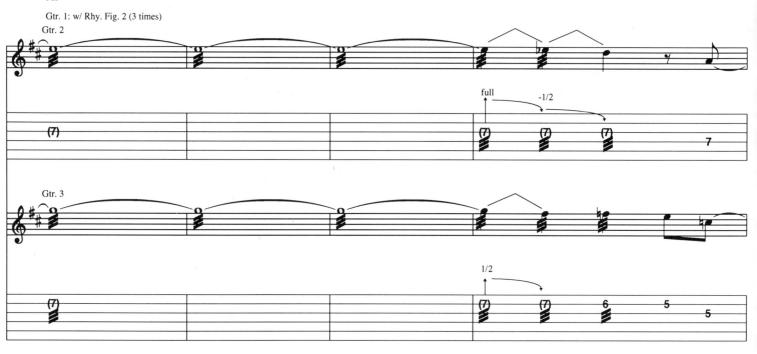

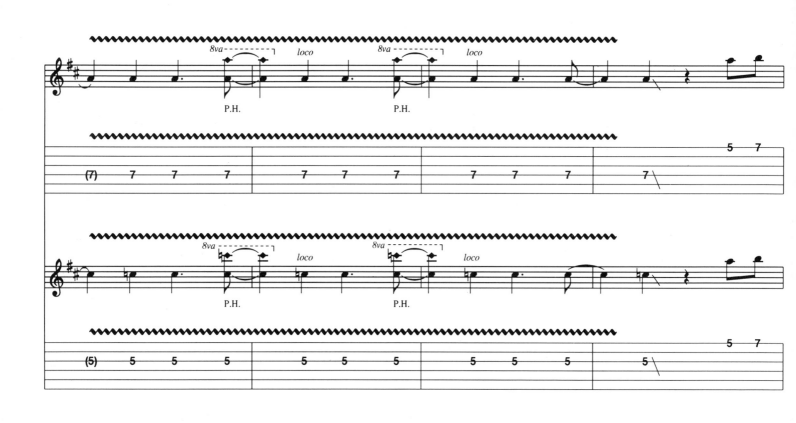

* Pre-bend w/bar - natural harmonic on 5th
string just behind 3rd fret. Slow release.

*On the 2nd and 3rd times through, Gtrs. 1 and 2 both play P.H.'s on designated notes, resulting in random harmonics sounding.

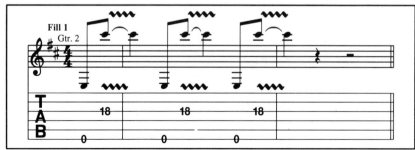

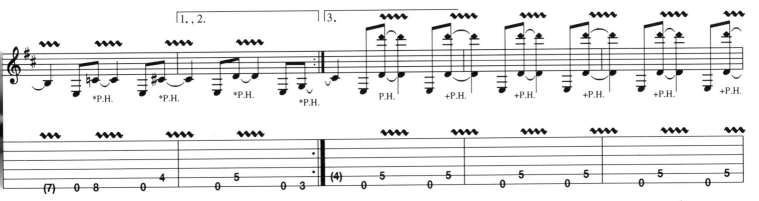

+ Gtr. 1 plays 1st P.H. of this section, then plays the regular notes with vibrato. Gtr. 2 plays each P.H. as written.

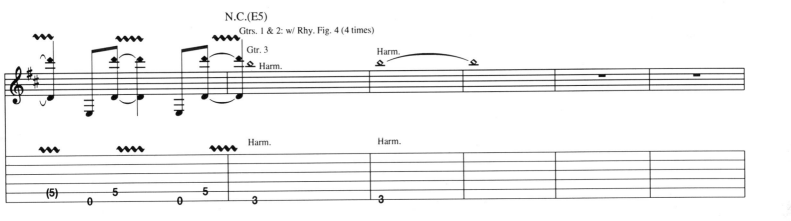

*This section features open harmonics played between the 1st and 3rd frets. B is on the 3rd fret, E is slightly ahead of the 2nd fret, G♯ is
slightly behind the 2nd fret, and so on. All tab fractions are approximate locations. Use maximum distortion and bridge pick-up for best results.

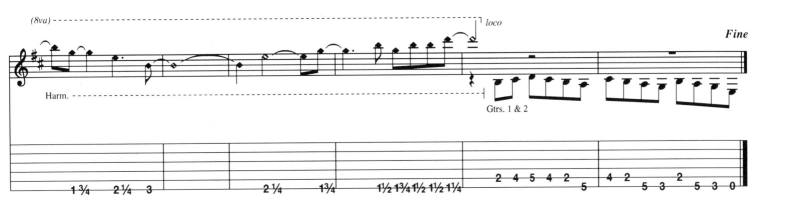

Waiting For An Alibi

Words & Music by Philip Parris Lynott

*All "♪" in Gtr. 2 rhythm part are quick, percussive strums, muted with the left hand and of no specific pitches.

Had ___ to say I told you,
Sad ___ to say I told you.

1st time only: I told you.

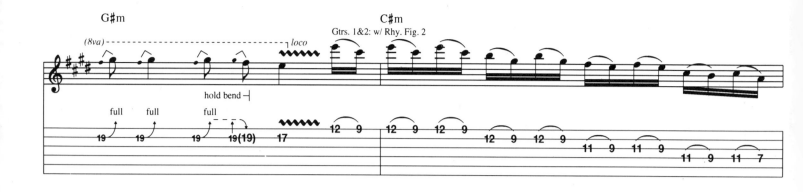

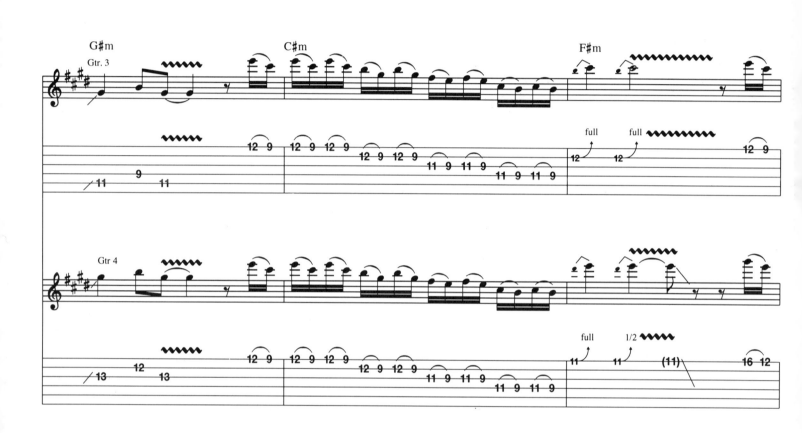

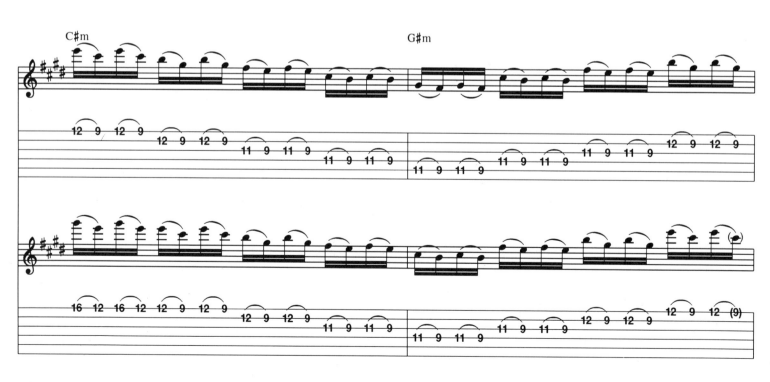

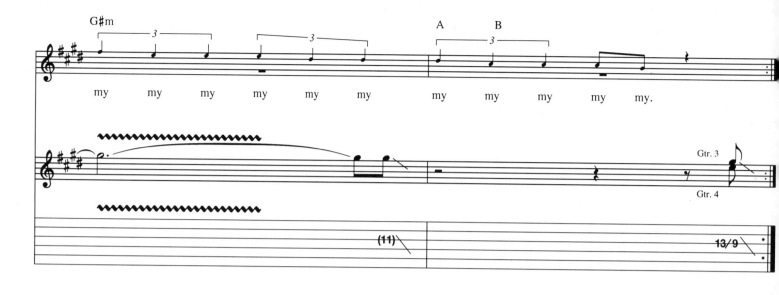

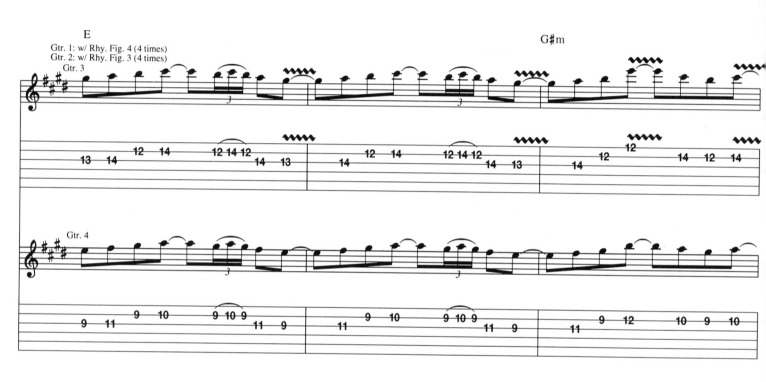

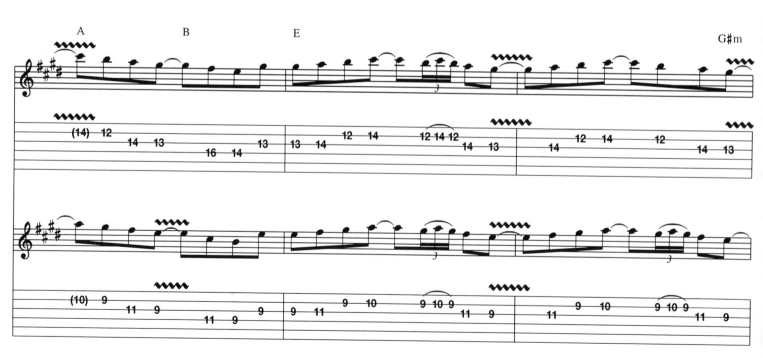

* natural feedback

Warriors

Words & Music by Philip Parris Lynott & William Scott Gorham

Verse

1. I am ___ a warr-i-or; I serve ___ the dark ma-chine.
2. I am ___ a mes-sen-ger; the mes-sage here you must know.

Los - ers are con - verts; all ___ flash past ___ on my sil - ver screen.
I am the warr - ior; I deliver the fatal blow.

Death is no ea - sy an - swer for those who wish to know. Just ask those who been be -
So fate will have to wait 'till time heals the scar. See my heart is ruled by

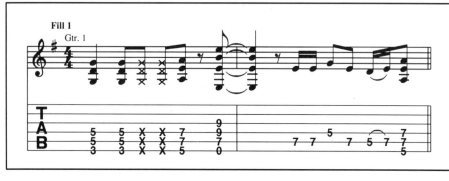

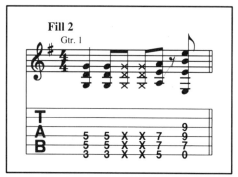

fore you
Ve-nus,

what fate the fu-ture holds. ___
and my head by Mars.

It ain't pret-ty.

Whiskey In The Jar

Words & Music by Philip Parris Lynott,
Brian Michael Downey & Eric Bell

Interlude

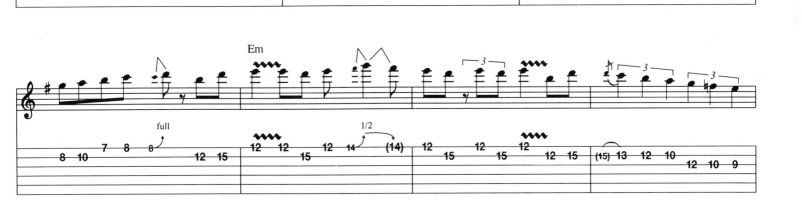

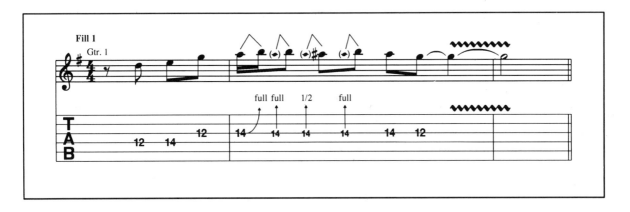

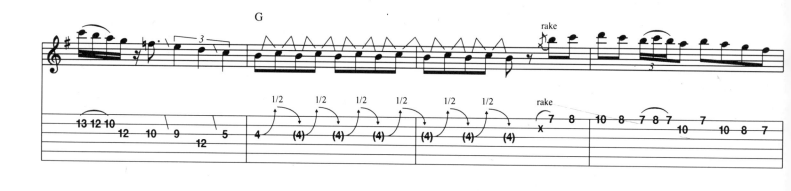

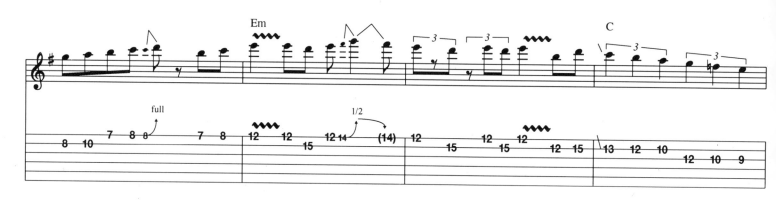

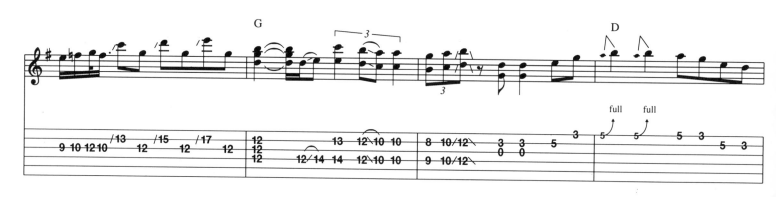

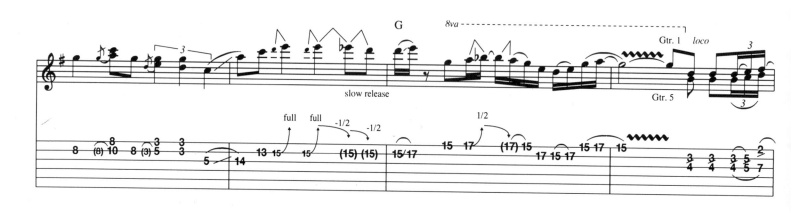

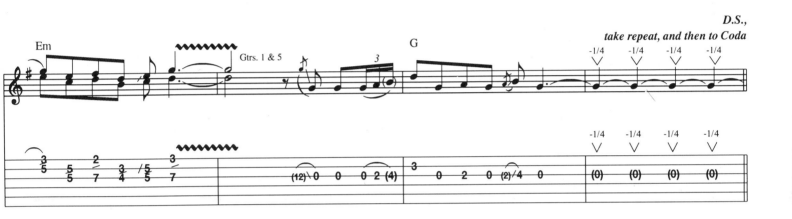

love, I love, _ I love, ___ I love __ now my - o - ah.

continue vocal ad libs.

Additional Lyrics

3. Being drunk and weary
   I went to Molly's chamber,
   taking my money with me.
   And I never knew the danger,
   for 'bout six or maybe seven,
   in walked Captain Farrell.
   I jumped up, fired off my pistols,
   and I shot him with both barrels.

4. Now, some men like a-fishin',
   and some men like a-fowlin',
   and some men like to hear
   the cannonball a-roarin'.
   Me, I like sleepin',
   'specially in my Molly's chamber.
   But here I am in prison.
   Here I am with a ball and chain, yeah.

Tablature & Notation Explained